Contents

Contents

bore for the sale barn

where the hogs ate the cabbage
vol 4

Wanda Morrow Clevenger

Writing Knights Press – Cleveland, OH

for Monte,
I have loved you wild

for
the boys
the girls
the grand
babies

bore for the sale barn
Writing Knights Press — Cleveland, Ohio

http://writingknights.com
@WritingKnights on Twitter, Instagram and Facebook

Images Belonging to: Wanda Morrow Clevenger

ISBN: 979-8-59925-352-5

Perigee Pearl

The moon was full of spoon-fed pearls looped
'round wedding day necks; and Steinbeck knew
of black and white and no in-between nooses.

Shakespeare coveted his. Keats wondered
at heroism. Banality claiming this moon doesn't
look much bigger than yesterday's retreats to
her trough. And

but for the mosquito who sampled the free wine bar,
I might have lingered to pay further homage with
an attentive thought.

In 1980, for ten dollars a woman dived for oyster;
a pearl plucked from its gelled host appraised
at ten dollars.

suicidal

8 thousand light years out
star WR104 was suicidal
close
her unstable barrel
aimed point blank

it could have gone one of
two ways

1 – no warning
a brilliant gamma ray
blast the last thing seen
as your eyes
vaporize

2 – no warning
a brilliant gamma ray
blasts the planet dark
photosynthesis blocked
plankton decimated
ice age--the last thing
seen as your eyes freeze

the devout were rooting
for the Mayan
were dead set
on revelation fire
called it
god using whatever evil
he could find in his arsenal

little deaths

some letters
on my keyboard
have lapsed into coma
the q and x and 3
and Cap Lock

I pound on their
little chests,
a distraught surgeon
desperate to
resurrect
their little deaths

the poltergeist
touch pad was
exorcised shortly
after startup—
its yellowish light
a 3-year reminder
of critical chaos

the guitar strum
of unopened document
further foreshadows,
mocks my mortality

another 24

at a reading at a senior center
with my comp lunch was narrated
the personal saga of the one wheelchair lady
who rattled from roll in to roll out as though
this memory marathon could snag her
another 24 topside

she parked next to me, still I didn't retain
much but how her son went to prison
and who knew it against the law to
look at pornography on a computer?

she shook to the bone in that wheelchair
shook when she ate when she drank when
she said the word pornography, and it's best
she didn't know exactly why he went to prison

she quieted down while I read a few poems
and a short story, and bless her anyway, she
was the only of the collective to make a
shrewd observation expressed with flawless
elocution—if you discount the pornography

truer lie

abandoned memory
brushed under the elegant oriental
is the truer lie; flawed disguise

An Owl in Residence

A night wind months before
frog thrum rock-a-byes baby,
carries on its breast
lost Jacob Marley.
And little else stirs this chill
but ruff and fluting.

For two decades an owl waits
with me for March tilt and
many weeks more before a crisp hoo
breaks within elm sequester. But

a mighty flotilla of green hummers
dogfight for nectar; dive bomb the cat
for fun; barnstorm dandelions
in broad strokes.

Athene hailed an owl in residence
a good luck omen;
one late autumn
I found a hummingbird nest
blown onto the road and keep this
talisman in a china tea cup.

Luck is lazy religion; a penny
picked off the ground. My allegiance
hails broader strokes.

no rhyme or reason

I keep logging on
to the wide world
and see purple paisley
painted posts
on how we are all
>here for a reason<

and wonder if those
posting pilfered prophecy
have considered
all the endless
convoluted angles

are the mass murderers
and rabid rapists and
tireless terrorists and
delusion dimwits
here for some tainted
saintly reason

some grand
"in the wider scheme
of things" propriety
a piddly peon
that is I can't
ever possibly
perceive

and sometimes
I see posts on how
there's hallowed reason
why some die while I didn't
and he didn't but
only by a thin ripple
in space time continuum

and there is no tidy
rhyme or reason
for the 200
way up there on
Everest

how Green Boots froze
sitting alone under
an overhang
until over 20 years
the wind lay his cold bones
down to rest, the mountain
making of him
a waypoint marker

Footnote:
Since 2014, Green Boots has been
missing, presumably removed or
buried.

Chucking Tar Clods

The blasted mutt first charged across half
the south field, madly barking, while I cleared sticks
from the back yard—an act of fair warning;
me ignorant of an exercised purpose. And keen

for a taste, it slipped in behind on the hard road
near our mailbox, quiet until a low growl grappled
my gut and I was seven cowered against a sister
at the school bus stop.

Grade school scaredy-cat now called wuss. But
on the other hand, he said, Blue Heelers are bred
to herd livestock. I looked a straggler; stragglers
don't stand a chance. And cornered

on the hard road I did fear snarl and tooth and
how tar clods chucked at its head only spurred
the blasted mutt. And swinging

a rolled magazine, I came close to fearless known
before Grandma's shepherd slipped in behind
the swing set for a taste.

songbirds

i.

black snakes hung
for two years in long
heavy loops on
heavy-leafed shadows
to steal summer song

lacking recourse,
the songbirds sacrificed

ii.

the massive crow
could feel tiny wings
batting against
its beak

feel enraged
pecks
prodding it from
branch to branch

the crow squawked--
the tiny winged
thing plummeted
into the brush

the crow dived
retrieved, rose

iii.

an hour passed and
the crow, harassed
through the timber
from out the timber
and back in,
felt harmonized
recourse
yet

Circus Flaminius

Not even Moses wrote the sin of Eve;
anonymous product
a 5th century wag of unjust finger, and
the brethren shout hallelujah at
Sodom and Gomorrah virgin sacrifice.

Now new charlatans circle for the kill;
televised Circus Flaminius
public stoning of woman's womb—
Kirk Cameron trips over his tongue.

Manufactured Avow

On the sink wall of the one stall ladies in Dairy Queen
is a framed calendar print—full on summer idyllic,
majestic purple mountain, mirror curtain and babble carpet—
with manufactured avow in Lucida across the bottom edge:
And God saw all that he had made, and it was very good.

I slid my bifocals down my nose, leaned in and squinted
through one-stall murky light
—the dinosaurs were missing, again.

father's day

sleeping in Sunday
your arm heavy
across my shoulder
where nothing else
mattered, not food
not drink

even the air stilled
so as to not mar
the moment

Refills

Girls who grow up without
a daddy leave a messy spill from
this broken glass say experts. And
maybe a kernel of truth pops for
those long loathing absentee
emotion; readily refilled in backseats.

Photo of Author 1973

Noise Makers

Not the first go round
the roughest though
back up to deadfall
the troops massed for
victory party cake
balloons streamers
—noise makers

indignation stands tallest
at the wrong complaint window
signed treaties of former fights
trampled in the fresh forge.

Nemesis

In dreams I'm never a child;
struck mute in the middle
no smarter or braver for the rewind

the white coats say dreams help us
make sense of the world; flying
through the mind unremembered

Sigmund saw what he wanted
—brimming symbols—but warned
of thinking too hard; sometimes, he said
a cigar is just a cigar

and white coats say we are made
paralyzed in dream; cats and dogs
chasing nemesis

I can only recall falling fast; mute
and no braver for the rewind.

A People

They called you falcon warrior,
your hundred thousand
moving 55 million cubics from
borrow pits upon brown backs to
erect earthen mounds.

One mound for birdman burial with
4 men missing hands and skulls;
and inside the mass dig is said
vertical fingers claw for air.

Along the narrow walkway, leaning
into the rail into eon—pungent
earthen-blanket brushed aside—
I marveled at shell shaped-wings
sanctifying surround atrocity; this
before liken culture demanded reburial.

A civilization outside written word, (twice)
vanished but for mounds and woodhenge
and blanketed bones of a people;
we can't know your name
so say Cahokia.

outside bird

if time physically stood
still then is at 6:50 AM
in the hum of electric fan
stir of heady bud;
bed covers world buoyant
with dim dawn with
a bird outside trilling

What Chaos Befalls

If discount could kill
my impudence made moot—
and might bedlam self-correct
the man has not grown infirm;

oh, but he tells the story from then
in raspy, animated detail
a brother riding piggy-back across the creek
dipping both under in orneriness,
down periscope;

the time makes him laugh
and clear eyes wake from wrinkled beds
while he shuffles along this rambling road,
neurons firing at will;

though bandaged from mishap
none question validity of
handing him car keys, again;

this is your wake-up call, I said
act now, before . . .
but I'm not blood in their ears—
a pesky gnat swatted away;

still mercifully arguable,
what chaos befalls these late days
is quickly forgotten once more.

twenty two under the seat

this side the town limit
strays ran
in mismatched band
breeding nuisance
to no remedy
until town council
said
load a BB-gun
and have a blast

the mongrels who took
the truck
knew exactly the payoff
lazed around a picnic table
for days
sniffing around
after dark

they abandoned the truck
on a back road
stripped of tools
tossed the keys
hightailed it
with the .22
from under the seat

duplicity

observe the swollen dame swarmed
by her pets given pet names;
perfected duplicity

observe how is readily rendered
an endless supply of royal jelly

When He's Not Home

Lately I've dabbled in paranormal
and kid psychics and celebrity ghost stories;
Ryan Buell's fearless warriors

sneaking whiskey fill in a Limoges teacup
at all hours—comparison shopping
on the down low

I heard a group investigated 19th century
Loomis House just down the road
with their ghost geigers; Judge Loomis
still in residence behaving but for
thunks and one recorded peek-a-boo

Monte grouses at the obsession
the sham I can't look away from;
he doesn't want to know what happens
when he's not home.

Junk

We never gave his junk a cutesie name, like
naming my boobs—Left and Louie—
because it seemed sophomoric back then, but
if I had given Bennie and the Jets a name
I'd have chosen something modest, like Eveready.

In Lincoln Park

Meet me in the park
he said
by the silver giraffe
kids sliding down the neck
 off the tail
 watch them sail;

follow the trail
of bee-thick clover
'neath a crepe paper sun
fashioned with pinking shears
and pollywog ears;

wear pink panties
he said
twirl a circle
show your lace
make that fanciful, funny face.

Sands of Jerusalem

I had never hated the sinner but
hated the cache of minor sins;
the outline of his head in the sand
—dismissed in angry sex

we weather like people do
when what waits is zealot diehard
and everything is futile under the sun.

longest

by 7 pm the silent auction hall was at capacity,
having expelled onto the lawn just as many smokers

the building smelled of hoodwinked hope
a Smith & Wesson went for 1400
a neon Stag sign for 600 to the same bidder
as the Bud sign for same;
2 kiddie picnic tables for same too

our bid was high on a pottery urn
donation to the cause
too often attended but yet
there they and we were again,
in silent barter

I waited in the car while the smokers smoked,
while Monte waited in line to claim his 150-dollar urn
and felt bad knowing her prognosis was sleep long
and longer until longest

I placed the urn on a bookshelf when we got home
and went to bed; in the morning we were told
she had by then gone to sleep

Kid Messiah

I met this foreign kid on a writing site amid the players
and parasites, Mark Elder saying check out this wild shit;
and the kid had eaten magic fishes and loaves in a parallel life
and stole the secret of turning water into wine.

He went by J.J. and his stuff read like manic monkey macarena
that he threw at us like a hungry fish hook, daring the players
and parasites to look direct into the sun.

He liked cheese, every cheese ever made. And it was entirely
impossible to dismiss his erratic prophecy
or cheese fetish for anything
short of the second coming.

One day he asked for money. I hadn't taken him for a parasite
so made a philistine joke. J.J. disappeared then into thin air.

monsoon season

    for-better can fast
    fade to worse
    --a downwind
    uphill upheaval
    clinging to a
    leaky rickshaw
    in monsoon season;

    pack accordingly

gray

a spatter gray
out the north field
trekked far
to my back door
handout
won't be shooed

desire for owning
furor best lent to
faithful
timmys and lassies

so many artful habitats
donated to auction,
birdcage last to go
—hardest to let go

and I am leery of this
gray under my porch
he makes himself
too much at home

14,035 days

legit for
14,035 days
he says we have
nothing in common
as though he's been
scientologized
morphed from
dead Koa wood
rendered rain-man
as to how we
got together
in the first place

I ignore the remark
a sinless observation
he's maybe right
he's maybe wrong

as is my way
I beg to differ

used books

farthest from the entry
of the used book store
are sorted the rare
volumes--a worth
I rarely can indulge--

diminutive bounds
immortalized in 1800s oils
impaled on the hands
of Victorian
quiet white lace
quaking chastity

in close proximity
I find instead, Millay's
perfectly preserved spine
priced for
self impalement

gut punch

there was a handmade doll
named Margaret
wearing a grass green
handmade dress
whom I often
bullied

the youngest of four girls
I knew even then
how to effectively
level a gut punch

Margaret disappeared
one day, probably
tossed out
when I wasn't home

I had no choice
in the event
didn't get to say
good-bye
or sorry
for being
a bossy little bitch

second and third hand

for Rosella

some on the short side was come by honest
same as recreating, for lack of reference
and means, what came before until means
bought store jam and the canner went
the way of brittle spider bundles in
basement corners

we keep those bits scavenged at estate sales,
looking even more a pile of second and third hand
in bright noonday,
to reanimate reference

Winter Graffiti

Sneakers rubbing inside rubber
boots sunk deep in snowed mounds
soaking pants and socks and shoes at very last
until we are spent from freeing
icicles from gutter spouts with
crispy mittens for numb-fingered graffiti.

Denim-tucked knee boots tediously carving
desire in a crystal field to read only
if named boys had wings to decipher our
Nazca plateau devotion.

Clogs tossed at the back door for
sloshing to the burn barrel in months
of muddy footprints recording more rain than snow
this weirdly warm winter.

every word

it is in the span
of uncensored
long together
long drive home
from lobster and
tall mango drink
meals
that fixes mete
of every word
I ever wanted
to say

roadside crosses

all those roadside
crosses, white painted
nailed plywood with names
sometimes and always
faded plastic flowers

once in a while you can
drive up on a
metal one
powder coated
with laser cut name
and date

you can't miss them
X marks the spot

we don't remark
about the crosses
but drive on up
or down the road
alive and relatively
well and think
how these crosses
are just big bright
arrows
pointing to well
preserved pain

as if Type 1 wasn't enough

borderline Randle
McMurphy masochism
drew me to the online
diabetes groups

those needle gurus
were veterans,
some since childhood,
they were spouting
percentages
and number slash numbers
glucose levels
MDI
BGL
ketones
bolus
lantus loading
–before or after sex?–
subtracting fiber
from carb
and pumps and
brands–glitches–cost–
warranty expectancy

there was moaning and
wailing about something
or something else
that no one had a
universal answer for
or ever would

and no one dared speak
of recipes or food per se,
food oddly verboten

when I mentioned
I was enjoying
some success
with inhaled insulin
some helpful Type 2
said using that stuff
would give me
cancer

three sides

a praying mantis female
while copulating
will dine à la carte on
her partner's head

upon finishing
every last bite
she releases him,
the disengaged carcass
falls to the ground
where the aedeagus
continues to pump
regardless

in male–female relations
love hate hunger
are three sides
of the same coin

Lesser Carnivores

Many a bird pan-fried
out on the farm
when meat was daily bread;
lard cradled flour-pat
light & dark
laced with S & P

ahead reports of
murderous intent
against
yoke-swaddled
relatives reborn

Araucana hens supplied
watercolor breakfast
and side income until
a famished fox
caught wind

—remarkable how
none denounce
the lesser carnivores.

Friendly Fire

Chrissie rhymes with pissy and hissy fit and coo-coo
for cocoa puffs and from what little I saw of her smiling
mugshot she sure could get her hackles up; whatever
you do, don't call her 'miss' (that makes her real mad) and
if you address her as 'missus' you better be wearing a cup.

I had seen this brand before, behind door #2, Medusa fresh
from the hair salon, way on back in the show me yours and I'll
show you mine days where getting snatched bald for sticking
your head out of your fox hole was considered friendly fire;

the admin banned her from the group, she whined on her wall,
some defamation thrown in for artistic integrity
—an objective observer rushed to console.

corsage

in the streetlight spatter
a knot of men
vie for her attendance

a flower wrist tattoo
makes up for
missed prom corsage

Easier Come

The managing editor of the local
print deemed newsworthy
claimed she did fair by me,
reciting an "up-yours bitch" policy,
and my complaint was forwarded
to the phantom publisher;

a twisted game of Monopoly without a
get out of jail free card where letters
to the editor are carefully selected for
a captive audience inside the trash can;

so I peddled my signed books for four
unadvertised hours, fluorescents playing
off old rhinestone brooches and new sequins
—just one degree shy of chic—
while re-reading Jason Hardung's
the broken and the damned
wishing I could toss down naked in the street,
didn't have to be a lady all the damn time;

behind the library stacks an audio book
quoted Bible verses while Hardung
promised to talk God up in one of his poems;

I got up to stretch my legs
remembering the sour-grape verse
someone I didn't know
had referenced me in, and reflected on
this easier-come brand of buzz.

realty on Mars

there is a bustling 400+
realty market on Mars

after all, it's only green
backs and those floating glass
sink bowl exotic marble
counter 4-head shower
12-ft. ceiling California shutter
gas fireplace 4-season room
whirlpool tub hibiscus
plant upgrades
will guarantee resale
when you're too old
to give a piss
in the coat closet
in-house outhouse

and there is always
another buyer
or two or twenty
chomping the bit
one agent tells another
or so they claim
in confidence
so you better get
your game face on

because it is a game
of who blinks first—
who wins who walks

it's a raging river
of dirty dish water
builder's brown
it's a high HOA with
no gazing balls or
zombie gnomes allowed
it's a 5-lane interstate
drag race
to buy two-ply

you aren't in Kansas
anymore, except
that this *is* Kansas
and you have crash landed
on Mars

on the day the roofers came

for Stan Barker

I don't write on
days when I hear
a friend up
and dies--too soon
and cliché

the roofers pound
I expect light fixtures
to crash down
walls to fall in

gray shingles drop
are gathered
away
ZZ Top's "Legs"
throbs from
an open van
a compressor makes
an intermittent frizz

I drink honey tea
I read social sympathy
I pay bills
the washer/dryer
agitates/spins
I chase dust

tomorrow
the roofers
will pound the last
fresh shingles on - I'll
look up and pretend
all is put to right

entomology

an endocrinologist
appointment
will bring on the mother
of bad moods
trigger PTSD and
brother you'd better
back the jack off
that whole week before
because it is puny
me against the
needle Nazis
and when you dare
fight back
you're branded:
difficult
emotional
batshit

and 9 months
of torture
doesn't make me
any smarter
about anything
except
female praying mantis
so brother if
you find issue
with a published poem
about female
praying mantis
you better expect
I'll take your
head off

bleed the presidents poor

pony-up a startup
grand
for a flying
Persian
and 4 years, 1 book,
one-half manuscript
later
the thing
sputters
onto the median
ingesting poems
and
vomiting
error reports

kick in another
half G
and watch profit
on paper bleed the
presidents poor

swear unholy
the proxy cursor
and the castrating horse
it rode in on

Love and War

Wanda has thirty-two years in, he confides saying;
his unprecedented shot
leaves a powder burn coming back around
if my response is too enjoyed—best if I just mouth
thank you

my tongue is bruised from biting it
I'm rubber
you're glue
everything you say . . .

the damage done wasn't fatal, just one peg of the pedestal
I used to bow before;
yet, I wish I could have watched this chivalrous stand
as a fly on the wall, compound eyes multiplying defeat
while my insides went limp, even with knowing
the body count doesn't change
and their war was never mine to win anyhow

Still, I love him for having my back
despite the hugely winding wait.

Under a Purple Neon Sign

A Gay Ball, reads a flier
from a stack of yellow
clippings.
Night to Remember:
Frank Westfall's Famous
Orchestra all the way
from Chicago, Illinois
for the Tarro grand opening;
never forgotten
Christmas Eve 1924

big ballroom, big names,
big nights and newcomers
destined for bigness
under a Quonset hut roof
seating for 800
capacity 2000
parking for 500
(and the math works)

Dominic Tarro was found
January 30, 1930,
on the Sangamon River bank
bound with wire
—prohibition bootleg sugar
Sicilian style silence
played out against

the hottest line-up this side
of St. Louie:
The Kansas City Nighthawks
Ted Lewis, Guy Lombardo,
Lawrence Welk, Ray Anthony,
Tex Beneke, Duke Ellington,
Count Basie, Sammy Kaye,
Wayne (The Waltz) King,
Kay Kyser, Benny Goodman,
Tommy Dorsey, Ray Charles,
Little Jack Little, Ike and Tina Turner,
Everly Brothers, Johnny Rivers,
Chubby Checker, Fats Domino
—famed for breaking the piano stool
with his jiggle bounce—and scads more;
then came rockers Turtles, Styx,
Foghat, The Guild

the rockers roughest
on Dominic's daughter
—late, no-shows, delays, refunds—
Joyce Tarro ambushed
in her home at 2 a.m.
carrying 3000+ in door take
taking 6 bullets
—Valentine's Day repeat massacre—
the Saturday in '76
I was in Florida missing the music

Under a Purple Neon Sign (cont)

the black wreath lifted
from the door
rowdy roller skates rounded
where we circle danced McCartney's
"Nineteen Hundred and Eighty Five"
on oilmopped wood now
piled in dusty flea market
rejects stacked to the balcony
the stage crammed with
antique overflow entombs
musician autographs on a back room
wall—burned to rubble on July 31, 2011

a news clip claims Al Capone
frequented the Coliseum
under a purple neon sign
in coal town Benld
and like all who entered,
he couldn't have imagined
what was to come.

bore for the sale barn

by my mother's age
they are dropping
like chloroformed flies
brothers, sisters, old
good friends
old acquaintances
old school mates

she tells me names
I don't remember
some I do

by my age
they are dropping
too, one despicable
disease after another

and I was
on that drop list
next but
shimmied free

my mother watches
me for signs of
relapse, she knows
she's on the drop
list next too
I read it in her eyes
when she tells me
names

we are
every one
just cattle
dropped, hid out
in remote
gullies,
bore for
the sale barn

we are all
just meat
on the hoof

Frank Zappa was right

you are what you is

the meek won't inherit
the earth, hornets will
burrowed in high rise
condominiums
hidden in plain sight
that one sentry
ready eager
for battle
that fatal
pheromone radar
bearing down

they make a mockery
our being, theology,
space station squatted
on our shed
on our magnolia branch

they know they
don't need a god
to create
orchestrate, obliterate
they are already
omnipotent

Wanda Morrow Clevenger wrote eight poems in a handful of months in 1974; thirty-four years later she returned to writing. She has since placed over 467 pieces of work in 158 print and electronic literary journals and anthologies.

In August of 2013, while compiling the manuscript for this book she fell ill with pancreatitis, further complicated by necrosis in the following nine months, and wasn't expected to survive. One year later, almost to the day, she sat down to finish *where the hogs ate the cabbage.*

She has her husband to thank for the title.

Other Books by Wanda Morrow Clevenger

@ WritingKnights.com

www.ingramcontent.com/pod-product-compliance
Lightning Source LLC
Chambersburg PA
CBHW070616160726
48003CB00005B/2304